WATCHBOY, WHAT OF THE NIGHT?

Watchboy,

What of the Night?

By **TURNER CASSITY**

WESLEYAN UNIVERSITY PRESS

Middletown, Connecticut

Some of these poems first appeared in the following journals, to whose editors grateful acknowledgment is made: *Emory University Quarterly*, *Kenyon Review*, *North American Review*, and *Poetry*. Poems that first appeared in the last named are these: "Any Year at Bad Irgwendo," "Astrology," "Aubade," "Calvin in the Casino," "Chronology," "A Clock with a Mirror Face," "The Coast at Grand Isle," "A Colony of Another Kind" (originally titled "The Quarter"), "Complaint of the Cafe´ Musicians," "Earrings for the Virgin," "East Side, West Side," "Epigoni Go French Line," "The Flying Dutchman," "The Gardens of Proserpine," "Grace at the Atlanta Fox," "Haitian Endymion," "Hotel des Indes," "In the Western Province," "Johannesburg Requiem I–IV," "Junker-Lied," "Love in Cincinnati," "The Lumber Baron," "Märchen," "A Message from Mother Goddam," "Nocturne," "Out of the Pit," "Pastoral with Ski Lift," "Period Piece," "A Serenade for the Vicereine," "A Song in Subtitles," and "Woman."

"Lines Written in Oregon," by Vladimir Nabokov, quoted herein, copyright © 1959 by Vladimir Nabokov and originally published in *The New Yorker;* reprinted from *Poems*, by Vladimir Nabokov (Doubleday & Company, Inc., 1959) by permission of the author.

"The Broken Men" and "Song of the Wise Children," by Rudyard Kipling, quoted herein, reprinted from *The Five Nations*, by Rudyard Kipling, by permission of Mrs. George Bambridge, The Macmillan Company of Canada Ltd., Methuen & Co. Ltd., and Doubleday & Company, Inc.

Library of Congress Catalog Card Number: 66–23920

Manufactured in the United States of America

First Edition

To the Old Hands

What was the world like, before it fell: was there great sorrow?
... No, there was a peculiar sadness in the air, a feeling of
hundreds of days leading up to this particular day, and every
now and then the breath of a change to come as when the
great airs of summer move under August trees ...

—OSBERT SITWELL

Table of Contents

RUDIMENTS OF TROPICS

OOM-PAH FOR OOM PAUL

EXTRALITY GO HOME

Haitian Endymion

What partial dark, inverting on the sea
A melon with a rind of indigo,

What shadow in that riper night beyond,
Will hide the final dark I face from birth,

Who in the create darkness now my skin
See uncreated nothingness to come,

And in the tomb of the mosquito net
Seek out a sleep that dreams itself enough;

Who sleep, and am the nude somnambulist
For whom the flesh becomes sufficient cause,

When, risen in a sky no longer night,
La Belle Diane sinks toward the dark she leaves,

And of my body, naught that will not die,
Conceives the crescent margin that is life.

Aubade

Spacing with dark the light that we evade,
The single shutter stripes the sun with shade.

A striate flesh upon a striate sheet,
You are your hair, eyes, mouth . . . and thus to feet.

Two staggered bodies, one these bands of light,
The other, parallel confines of night,

You are in one self cosmos paced with sleep,
Chaos in whom fragmented rhythms keep,

And though one dream of order, when he mates
He is a chaos that perpetuates.

Momently, on these squares of swept rattan,
Our lizard *voyeur*, wearying of man,

Debates if he will circle, or will not,
The microcosm of the chamber pot.

And for the little time that he delays,
And in their far-out, citronella daze

His small familiars the mosquitoes dart
But do not strike—lie near me but apart.

As fever and as carrier, as force,
As loss, love soon enough will run its course,

Through sweat, through cramp, to be in its last breath
Receptacle, evacuation, death.

Teatro Amazonas
(Manaos)

Mosaic sidewalks phase the downcast vision,
And where it lifts, the solid dome has pulse—
As if that after-image, wholly motion,
Unfettered structure from the space it fills;

As if the silent house, its lush imprudence,
Were image only: focus, in pure void,
Of such bent rays as cultures in decadence
Fan outward to excite the dark they dread.

Extreme response bright in the heart of darkness,
Its awkward, beaux-arts force unworn by years,
The ornate folly conjures, all uniqueness,
Its belle époque of rubber millionàires.

Is it illusion that, to caned seat bottoms,
A sweating Bernhardt droned the chill Racine?
Illusion too, that ferried here as totems,
European singers, un-divine,

Unvaccinated, died of yellow fever?
Or have mirage and structure one live base:
Mute caryatids on whom rest forever
Art, folly, wealth, and the clear insights of ease;

Who, bearing still each headstone of their burden,
Solicit drop by drop the sticky trees;
Who know, how when the saps of nature harden,
Whips seek in time another in its place;

And who cannot know, how, for those who wield them,
It is enough that on brute darkness, rows,
One color, specify which forces yield them;
Until the spectrum and the blood oppose,

And dim all color downward. Red . . . magenta . . .
Full darkness: when the builders struggle home,
And what was exclave ends as irredenta;
When caryatids rise and heave the dome.

A Message from Mother Goddam

Scattered our smoke, uprooted now the poppy:
What dream, Taipan, did your delusion copy,

That as in a dream the yellow millions
Should on these mud flats raise you stone pavilions?

Until that city, still not real, seem wholly
Their pleasure dome to ease your melancholy,

And on the Bund, in solace of your boredom,
The jerking rickshas pull their weight of whoredom.

What vision seeks here to preserve forever
Each gleam, each mist of this imagined river?

Mirage or water, there, at humid dawnings,
The idle gunboats let out canvas awnings;

Marshaled at evening in the White cantonments,
Your putteed garrisons ward old alignments.

It is yourself they guard. When, dream unshaken,
You sleep on, and the dreamless sleepers waken;

When, riven with a dream's withdrawing thunder,
The treaties crumble and the ports go under,

Where then is your identity—whose vesture,
Substance, essence, all vanish in a gesture;

Whose future, retrospective and uncertain,
Is this illusion through a beaded curtain.

La Petite Tonkinoise

I am not person, and am not opinioned.
I exist as I have been companioned.

You create me. Legionnaire or Viet,
I was your Somewhere East of Cigarette;

As I shall be, for grown-up Terry, beady
Eyed as ever, real-life Dragon Lady—

Anna May Wong, or, Soong once more, and young,
A not so avaricious Madam Chiang.

All pirate, you, the lanky, latest comer,
Jump-booted, trample the eternal summer;

Pausing only when, like any drab,
I cycle past you on a pedicab.

As the tight skirt scissors, so the ankle hinges.
While it does, no other change impinges.

Yet I and wheel, meek where your glance is hurled,
Combined, were Fortune, Empress of the World.

Were each reversal. I that stony bosom,
Parachute and you the broken blossom;

Who, even now, hear in the anklets' ring
No warning—only jada, jada, jing

Jing jing.

Calvin in the Casino
(He apostrophizes a roulette ball)

Sphere of pure chance, free agent of no cause,
Your progress is a motion without laws.

Let every casuist henceforth rejoice
To cite your amoralities of choice,

By whose autonomy one apprehends
The limits where predestination ends;

Where the Eternal Will divides its see
In latitudes of probability,

And the divine election is obscured
Through being momently and long endured.

It is obscured and is rejustified,
That stands fulfilled in being here denied,

Lest its caprice should lead the mind to curse
A biased and encircling universe,

Or its vagaries urge us to reject
That one same Will which chooses the elect.

OOM-PAH FOR OOM PAUL

Day long the diamond weather,
The high, unaltered blue—
—RUDYARD KIPLING

The Flying Dutchman

The facing seasons change in storm,
And I through time's long equinox
Must challenge darkness at its norm,

To seek always an unseen Crux,
And by that love I would beseech
Mock still the entity which mocks.

Though, in the land I do not reach,
The season keeps, and in blue skies
Blue grapes hang, swollen each to each—

Condoned already, compromise
Steals blue by blue the summer's truth.
Eternal equinox must rise:

Fruit out-of-season draw the mouth
Unebbing love no more assails;
The Cross set clouded in that South
Where, all unchallenged, Hell prevails.

In the Western Province
(Stellenbosch, 1960)

On autumn streets, in thinning shade,
Deep gutters shine with mountain water;
And on the stones that bridge them, staid
Hesperides in orchard clutter,

Mulattresses sweep off the leaves.
Mulattoes, gutters, arbors, gables,
Each year re-create, as the sheaves
Create elsewhere autumnal fables,

A true autumnal; add, each fall,
Bright days that face one harvest only,
Ripening toward no germinal
The sterile fruit transplanted vainly,

To harden seedless into gold,
And have, though all its taste be metal,
Such luster as will take and hold
And flatter, howsoever brutal,

The race whose fetish it becomes,
Until the mirror is the treasure;
Until the sallow image numbs
The blood's response, and is the measure,

Prospect, and face of privilege;
A last apartness, finally cruel.
With all compassion numb, with each
Vain myth inbred beyond renewal,

Apartheid stares in classic pride.
Youth, knowing what the mirror utters,
Will not hear now, on either side,
Time running out in darkened gutters.

Märchen
(Southwest Africa)

We contemplate, *Fräulein*, a land so dry
This water in itself is Lorelei;

And put your comb to whatsoever use,
It is the tank and windmill that seduce.

Divided skirt, bush jacket, boots. Though sex
Expire in local color, yet will *heks*

Be *Hexe* still; be challenge, be response,
Of myth to drouth, of song to Afrikaans.

Undress and with that water merge. Resist,
And I am nakedly a *Narzissist.*

Woman
(From the Afrikaans of Elisabeth Eybers)

The lesser seasons pass in wide,
Sure exodus across a land
Where she retains the spring, whom love
Exalts one season out of time.

Hate and destruction fix elsewhere
The standards of the night. In her,
Whom blood, whom struggle also wait,
Peace and well-being echo still.

The horseman halts, the sickle lowers;
And in the distance of her glance
Death measures his dominion's end.

She summons, ward of timelessness,
All futures in the faint reflex
Of life forever re-begun.

Out of the Pit

Today, the Kimberley Mine is surrounded by a high wire fence. The fence has been there ever since late in the last century, when a man committed suicide by throwing himself into the crater. The city authorities were never able to retrieve his body, and some people say that every now and then it rises to the surface and floats about.   —EMILY HAHN, *Diamond*

At Kimberley the sundered clay
Gives up in fee, to the broad light,
This recompense for light held prey
In the strait crystal; gives up, white
With time, the crystal's parallel:
Clay straitened in a perfect shell—

Clay that, grown merely isolate
In death, was once particular;
In its distinction, obdurate.
This mine returns us what we are;
The suicide, the diamond,
They are ourselves. We are the bond

In whom unite specific fire
And its obscuring earth; for whom
Can serve neither a common pyre
Nor the compound clay of the tomb.
For severed elements this rite:
Earth out of earth, earth come to light.

JOHANNESBURG REQUIEM
(To settings by Kurt Weill, Friedrich Holländer, et al.)

I
Gold

Below us, in the shafted ground,
Set charges shatter into sound,
And over us, in shattered light,
Thunder prolongs the dynamite.

If we, on balconies of glass,
Can, unmoved, feel those tremors pass;
Can feel no shame for ton on ton
Of gold so obdurately won,

Neither need they who in dark earth
Exact what has for them no worth
Remember how in darkened skies
The brilliant veins unbidden rise.

II
By the Waters of Babylon

We serve, by tribute of a tongue not ours,
A Mammon which ignores us; toward whose greed
We raise blind walls, and from whose very towers
We search in vain the land that they succeed:

A land in which the gentle thrust of rain
Bears up the sky of summer, and where dust,
In winter, turns above dry sheaves of grain.
Beside the outspanned oxen, red as rust,

The white tick birds divest a stolen blood,
Whose certain presence is their freedom lost.
So, in a blood we have not understood,
Are we as well the parasite, the host;

Who mingle, in these alien arteries,
The indigenous we scorn, on which in turn
We force our passions, our posterities.
It is a single fire in which we burn.

Upon the altar of that coming flame,
Toward the variety of our own vice,
It is the simple birthright we disclaim,
It is identity we sacrifice.

III
Homage to Rider Haggard

Sundowners and the setting sun
Have made the loss, the losers one.

In amber whisky, amber light,
Inaction and the act unite,

As, promise of the land they fail,
Its last inheritors, still hale,

Still arrogant, assume by youth
A future no more theirs in truth,

Effecting, of their wicker chairs,
The burden that the Black Man bears,

And of the green tile flooring, Earth:
Apportioned them for race and worth,

Who are themselves their own ideal,
Power of a state no threats repeal,

No pity blurs, no fact distorts—
Platonic myths in khaki shorts;

And who will in a little while
Be gross, dim shadows in that tile

Which must reflect as well, unseen,
The waiters who have always been,

And ceiling fans whose cycling shade
Impels the time that else were staved.

IV
Watchboy, What of the Night?

Do you envision, in this night
Which is your being and your end,
The outworn night you half renounce,

Or do you, where your sidewalk fire
Is hearth and future, guard the light
So lately come, so hardly kept,

Signaling now from every street
The one response: unchange, content;
As if the omen were itself

Its own denial, and the man
Who watches in the night were all—
Protector, danger, oracle.

A Serenade for the Vicereine
(Durban)

Memsahib, let the world's defection
Be, in this other, resurrection.

Let these shores where still is homage
Raise up again your medaled image,

To sanction, by viceregal presence,
The vacant forms of our senescence:

Genteel petitions, Rugby, *Emma.*
(Houseboy, cookboy, driver, amah;

None of them sullen, none unruly.
Here is lower than the coolie.)

Here are the slow, spent days of remittal—
Become, unearned, the raj in little,

Where the surfboards nick the breakers,
Where new stock issues find no takers;

And where the sea, as in subpoena,
Cries, too familiarly, "Edwina . . ."

Servant Problem
(Johannesburg)

High wind across the mine dumps, and in shining air
The shining grit. In winter sunlight, lemon-clear,
A million small reflectors settle on the stair.

Indifference in his mind and push broom in his hand,
The flat-boy, function less than ornament, unmanned
In being always boy, malingers; bits of Rand,

Ignored, remain. Shall I submit or shall I scold?
The ornament is lame and sixty-five years old.
The not especially unsettled dust is gold.

The Gardens of Proserpine
(1897, 1962)

Iron queen of uncreations
    And of aborted birth,
Her pedestals new nations,
      Her form benchmarks the Earth.
        With all life disregarded,
        And greed no more rewarded,
        Her alias discarded,
    She concedes Death his worth.

If life renews without her,
    And Death finds there new need,
Death was too long about her
      That she should now be freed.
        Lace mantle ordered rightly,
        The tiny crown set tightly,
        Her double chins unsightly,
    She counts the alien seed.

EXTRALITY GO HOME

Do you recognize that clover?
Dandelions, *l'or du pauvre?*
(Europe, nonetheless, is over).
—VLADIMIR NABOKOV

Poseidon in the Fountain

My faint shadow, turned with the chilly sun,
Has for its hours the colors of these tiles,
Dry to the wind, dry to the spinning leaves.

I who exemplified the timeless sea
Am grown, in season of an arid cold,
The gnomon of an accidental dial.

Unendingly, I bleed upon this stone
A blood of bronze, who had a blood of salt.
In one last enclave, narrowing with winter,

I mourn the bright dominion thrown on summer.

Le Bassin Vert

(From the French of Henri De Regnier)

Goddess transposed from water into bronze,
No more an element, you rust toward earth—
A barren vine enlaureling your hair,
The urn your source grown silent in your hand.

Perfidious, the water mirrors whole
That shadow which all things in it become.
The fluid mirror where your shadow falls
Would be inversion of the sky it mocks.

Forever green, the fountain and the lawn
Are framed alike by hedges and by stone.
Equivocal and measured, each is life.

And in the water, see, as in the grass,
How, turn for turn, gold understudies gold;
The dead leaf parallels the turning carp.

Hotel des Indes
(The Hague)

The bell-pull summons, toward my ease,
Mnemosyne as Javanese.

Inscrutable from sole to head,
Two chambermaids turn down the bed;

While, pyramiding in my eye,
The contoured ricefields siege the sky,

And where their stepped horizon ends,
An even sugar reascends.

Forever, by those porches, leaves
Extend the shade of tilted eaves,

As if, in our pajamaed noon,
Inherent night, through form undone,

By shadow particled, were stayed;
As though event were so betrayed,

And those who with a Dutch wife lie
Embrace there immortality.

Bowing double, the maid retreats.
It rains till midnight, then it sleets.

Dutch wife.   A rest for the iimbs, used in beds in tropical countries, esp. in the
Dutch East Indies.   It consists of an open frame of rattan or cane, or often a
long round bolster stuffed with strips of paper.
—*Webster's New International Dictionary*, 2nd ed.

33

A Somewhat Static Barcarolle
(Amsterdam)

Neutral and dull, the bricks that serve as shores
Enforce their color on the channeled water;
And if a distant movement, as of oars,
Has made that mirrored brick, its mortar scatter,
Now, as the soon abated force goes slack,
A leveling inertia lays them back.

Surface on surface to a depth of peace—
How little stirred to be so far from stagnant!
As if reflection and its slow release,
Its visions idly on that water regnant,
Themselves were substance and renewal; beat
Or silence; action, and the act complete.

As if our shadows, lengthening below,
Received us bodily to calm, to vision,
Always to rock with lifted oars; where, low
Beside the mirror, sense and its precision
Give to the arching sky, the dormered town,
A motion one brick up and one brick down.

Junker-Lied
(Schleswig-Holstein)

More than myself (estate, degree),
I discipline my world to me,

For whom the viewpoint fills the view;
For whom all things become these few:

Four pinnacles and four clear ponds,
A quartered sky that corresponds;

The charted cattle, maps of peace,
And white ellipses which are geese.

If, in the dream's contempt of truth,
A goosegirl first is swan, then youth . . .

Awakened, would he see in mine
Seducer's eyes and base design,

Or only see what he may know,
That evil's grace is not to show.

Could he distinguish, did he try,
Which is the eyeglass, which the eye.

East Side, West Side
(Lübeck)

With Baltic accents and with Slavic faces,
Exiles take up tickets, pick at laces.

East Prussian, *Gräfin*, *Graf*, you now are these:
Conductors, washroom warders, seamstresses;

And speech and blood will sound you, if you listen,
Their mingled backwash of the *Drang nach Osten*.

If Elbing and if Danzig, Aryan once,
Lie mute in Poland's clustered consonants;

If Königsberg, the matrix of pure reason,
Is the Kaliningrad of mappers' treason,

Here, bordered by the unmapped gains of time,
A shrunken Hansa tolls the bankrupt home,

To learn, who were its furtherers, its creatures,
How dominance makes vain all other futures;

To see above steep streets—conclusive, plain—
Declining rooflines graph the sectored rain,

Till every prospect plots the same declension,
And you are placed. Your one choice comprehension,

The ample choice of youth to this decreased,
You face upon you the Slavonic East.

Any Year at Bad Irgendwo

In ruts of wheel chairs and the pocks of crutches,
The *Kurhaus* honors its decrepit duchies.

I tuck your lap robe, wheel you into status.
On Fridays one can take the waters gratis.

You are a sometime cygnet, deaf and gouty;
I am a suave young man of two-and-forty.

As *émigrée* and second generation,
We form a Tsarist, Russian-speaking nation;

Embody, in the course that we maneuver,
Fixed idea and the unmoved mover.

You've pawned the hearing aid, redeemed your brooches.
Counterrevolution, sound reproaches.

The columns glisten and the fountains trickle.
I stoop to comment, and your egrets tickle.

They, ornamental to their near extinction,
In life survive from danger into sanction.

We, sanctionless and soon unique, shall, senile,
Exhibit the end of sheer panache; who, meanwhile,

In every mineral of each hot water,
Can taste how being *démodé* is bitter.

Pastoral with Ski Lift
(Garmisch, Summer 1936)

Above us, dwindling into fiction,
One self-repeating crucifixion.

Inconclusive, bright-lit air;
Sailplanes it will part and pair—

Now omens, now the runes of order.
But in these fields, whose vagrant border

Still is what cold stream, no pain
Exhales from the dividing grain

Save that we read into it. Neither,
In our wingless lower ether,

Has any sign its high import;
Nor, in the symbols they distort,

Is evil fixed, or good endemic.
Sung words, in echo, bring their comic

End to Movement and to Youth;
As if its marchers, who, sheer faith,

Pass yet with banner raised, with quiet
Steady tread, in meager riot

Broke step once and then were mute.
As if the staid life they refute

Held nonetheless; and they, stout sutures,
Had only peace-filled, farming futures;

Where Jew and where Mercedes Benz
Have each their star and each their rents,

And where in fleeting, local visions
A total state has its omissions.

War has its compensations, *Kreuz*
Its variant the *Hackenkreuz*.

The Afterlives of Count Zeppelin

Inflated, yet elliptical, of epic size,
What great Teutonic riddle hangs there in the skies?
It is the *Graf von Himmel*, bearing far from Jews
And postwar debt true Germans on eternal cruise:
Teachers of counterpoint, and, wives in braided locks,
Cherubic manufacturers of cuckoo clocks;
Ex-Kaiserin, Big Bertha, other Krupps, and—*echt*—
A mid-air cellar tanker planes refill with *Sekt*.
For cabin class, a *Turnverein*, a skating rink,
And fourteen cabin boys, to hum them Humperdinck.
Moreover, in the steering gondola, her odd,
Stiff navigator may, conceivably, be God.

Below him there? The flaming skeleton he passed?
That is the *Graf von Hölle*, burning at the mast:
Our instant crematorium. Zigeuner, Slav,
Observe that transportation of the do-not-have;
The gas-fed *Götterdämmerung* of such as die
Unsuited for the great Bayreuth there in the sky;
Who, in the framework of the blazing hull, burned dark,
Pursue the buckling doors; who end as hurried sparks,
And know that in the dummy gondola, ramrod
To the end, hand on the valves, their fellow spark is God.

Epigoni Go French Line

Egalitarian and full of plastics,
S.S. France, efficient, safe, and banal.
Mirrors double in the English Channel.
One reflection has her own statistics;
One has patently an extra funnel.

She, that other, follows where the real
Distorts her; just below the water, just,
But only just, describable—her past
Already idiom, her loss detail.
Imperfectly, the structured meaning lost

And connotation gone, hers, nonetheless,
Prevail. Time is the steward of décor.
In auctioned fittings that no longer are,
Persists the image that forever is:
Ease, class on class, and in the distance, war.

Meanwhile, if enamel, glazes, metal
Bear the mark of Cain, here, being human,
It lends them what the *France* can never summon.
Simply, well aware it may be fatal,
Luxury is drive toward the uncommon.

It is for those crystal decks their caption,
Seal, or birthmark; it is where in sudden,
Brief incests of conspicuous consumption,
Action mannequins, or Wallis Simpson,
Meet fortune hunters in the Winter Garden.

It is the stainless steel piano, closed.[1]
Its motive of the jagged chromium,
The frozen lightning flash, forever posed
Above what portal, brands on whom they used
The shaping will and realized extreme.

And though internment, auction, fire, and scrap
May wait it, they are such *frisson*, such fear
As give it edge. To grace it with death pure,
To spare it, thus, graffiti of the troop-
ship, "Kilroy took his social vengeance here,"

Elective fire seems less than ever Hell.
The Channel clouds; the ships merge utterly;
Our faith now is in the *France*, for good or ill.
But when the bored forsake the guarding rail,
The life preserver, spotlit, still reads *Normandie*.

1. The stainless steel piano was actually aluminum, and was on the *Hindenburg*,
    not the *Normandie*. This is known as poetic license.

ISLAND SOLITUDES

In sickness, the sight of an island
(even a very small one) is generally
more fatal than the view of a continent.
—JOSEPH CONRAD

The View from the Caribe Hilton

Entire in color, undefined in form,
The partial rainbow walls the far-off storm,

Confining, by its wide, unfinished arc,
A lightning-lessened but recurring dark,

Whose tardy thunder comes uncertainly
To break the second thunder in the sea.

The perfect arch we still anticipate,
That might, before its pure fire abate,

Render eternally worth while that night
Which is to follow, here does not see light.

The massive prism of the lifting rain
Leaves on that farther rain no unflawed span,

And color that is covenant no more
Lets through at length darkness it cannot shore.

Earrings for the Virgin

Beneath Our Lady's wooden lobes
Let us imagine twinkling globes,
That of those painted suns, her eyes,
New solar systems improvise,
And create, toward no son to be,
A heaven that is wholly she.

The older heaven, slow to come
And heavy then with tedium,
As pedestal for beauty's pall
Is witness first of beauty's fall;
And thus also, Our Lady's gems
Are both comments and requiems.

From the immortal mother gone
There comes now, queen in time alone,
A Virgin mortalized by pride;
One who might yet be deified
As woman only, jewelry
The emblem of her vanity;

One who remembering no more
Of heaven than we knew before,
Might die at last as we shall die,
Uncertain of eternity
And certain not to find in wood
The short perfections of the blood.

Henceforth, as likeness of that state
Death will no more anticipate,
And of its still-entreated love
One symbol not itself enough,
Our Lady of the Pierced Ears
Must barrenly sustain our years.

Cemetery
(San Juan)

Between the sea wall and the sea,
Time's lessening destruction braves
The dissolution still to be.
The sealed and designated graves
Face toward the undermining waves.

And if that later, traceless death
Lays bare at last a skeleton,
To round the little world of breath
With blank environments of bone,
It is a ravage all condone.

We who are selfishly aware
The known dead have with them our grief
Who have our youth, will not despair
To see cast on the pitted reef
Dead whom no context will retrieve.

Don Juan and the Painted Fan

Winds in these patios we range
Last out a year that does not change.
The currents which your hands dispose
Are of a world that comes and goes;
That in a narrow darkness locks
Its pleated streams, its crinkled rocks;
Or spreads before the ravished eye
Landscapes of cloth and ivory,
And maidens who would flee once more
Ribbed lovers whom they touched before.

But since you could not if you would
Resume with them lost maidenhood,
Or see a lover rise still fresh
From the embrace of silken flesh,
Remember that our own estate
We cannot quite unconsummate;
Wherefore, to bare your hidden eyes
Were hardly further compromise.

Return to their divided dark
The bloodless forms age cannot mark.
Youth, finite as their sectioned sky,
Contracts about us till we die,
And seen through spaces of your fan,
I am dismembered flesh, not man.

The Coast at Grand Isle

The land develops, at its end,
This flatness men cease to defend.

No fill restores, nor sea wall guards,
Bare, ebbing sand no life retards,

That measures, on the double gray
Of sky and gulf, the space we stay

And is the land we occupy.
Horizon dark beyond our sky,

Hurricane strong beyond our strength,
When you subject us, when at length

We scoop in sand the flooded grave,
We learn what false recourse men have

With death—who, into silt dispersed,
Ebb with the tide, and are reversed.

IN THE LAAGERS OF BURGHERDOM

We have forgotten the look of light,
We have forgotten the scent of heat.

They that walk with shaded brows,
Year by year in a shining land . . .
—RUDYARD KIPLING

Love in Cincinnati

In comfort, soot and snow lose each their rigors.
Our backdrop fits *Bohème*, but we are burghers;

And through our windows, in that moving stipple,
Go past the figures of the not quite people:

Intermittent, partial, pointillistic—
No more a likeness than if we, bold, plastic,

Entire, unmade them by our mere example;
Than if our bodies (counting house, not temple)

Housed yet a spirit they, for all their motion,
Cannot warm. Who treasures inhibition,

Here, may find it, in its late expressions,
Unearned income that supports the passions;

Find also, laying-by whatever wounded,
How middle age returns it all compounded.

Accruing time, of what unlikely mortar,
Has built us thus a burgess Latin Quarter;

Of red brick rectitude and iron repression
Improvised this gaslit indiscretion,

And placed about us, linked to love's warm center,
The populated streets we now must enter.

Period Piece

Leather helmet, lifted goggles,
Out of the cockpit Lindbergh struggles—

Henceforth, accident or plan,
Anything but Everyman:

Icarus intact, all Paris
His, and, his to be, an heiress;

While the honest press chants still
"Ambition, self-reliance, will."

Yet, goggles lowered, helmet fastened,
Photographed, he so is chastened;

Grown a skull, thus put upon,
He must himself cry Jedermann;

As though foreseeing loss, the Axis,
Graduated income taxes;

Seeing corporate, bland thoughts
Which are the minds of astronauts,

And how one hears an honest press
Chant "Teamwork, peace, togetherness."

The Complaint of the Café Musicians

For my mother and my grandmother

Oasis less than mausoleum—life, and tomb—
The hothouse palms divide us from the dining room;

And we, a sort of living death on union scale,
Are its subliminal concern that life prevail:

An anti-Muzak not of spheres.
                              If piped-in life
Created, if the tape were fecund, all our strife

Were only one more time lag hardly felt as need;
But while the prime, crude movers still are gut, hair, reed—

We share their stigma; who are by their limits bound,
And must of atavism make a striving sound.

If advance leaves us mute, so, in time's backward dark,
Did Vitaphone.
                  The ornate tango faded, the stark

Ten Cents a Dance is one with Rudy and with Ruth[1]
Out there in Nowhereland; and we who in our youth

Could fake a leitmotif for Pola-Negrity,
Have in old age a lucid, mild integrity:

The certain confidence of those who keep one course,
And know the rosined bow of music at the source,

Though in the air-wick air one hear, on tape, a screed
Familiar as *Intolerance*, as old as *Greed.*

1. Miss Etting was at this writing (1964) still very much alive, but resident in
    Florida.

Grace at the Atlanta Fox

Whenever, in that ceiling sky,
Familiar clouds once more go by,

And in the restrooms, far below,
One half the lamps of Islam glow;

When, overweight but overawed,
Undying Grace, eternal Maude,

Once more are en rapport—are one—
With Myrna Loy and Irene Dunne

(Irene as essence, Maude; *Ur*-Myrna:
Now the new star Annapurna,

Nepalese and thick of tongue);
Or when, pure movie, pure, brave, young,

The Foreign Legion dare and do,
Each year is 1932;

Pre-Eleanor, pre-war, pre-Fala;
Time as place: the Garden of Allah,

Near whose entrance, chill with Freon,
That time's great sign resists still neon,

To be through Moorish, Hoover nights
This fugue of incandescent lights;

As if to make some statement yet;
As if the tan brick minaret

Were point and counterpoint; not theme,
But theme to be, that when the dream

Maude dreams is ours, and we too nod,
States then "There is no God but God . . . "

Of Heaven as Production Number

Perspective false and canvas full of tears,
The painted backdrop terminates real stairs;

And toward that point at which they vanish, paint
Or hole, an act of faith impels, not saint,

But mediocrity. Sure his trite steps
Somewhere will be writ large, a dancer taps

Intent as though some new dimension yawned.
It yawns. There on the screen, the backdrop pawned,

A black and white aurora throws with ease
A staircase of immense piano keys;

Ascending which, in top hats, nothing more,
Pure-tonic chorus girls tap out the score.

Angelic Evas in angelic curls,
Angelic Topsies in melanic pearls,

And in the center, dancing as he did,
The unimproved and undone hominid:

Machine-writ large upon the starry void,
Yet flattened thereby into celluloid;

Who, in the round, by slowly failing strength,
Learned there is only width and breadth and length,

To be dispelled one stairstep at a time;
However often still he may, in time,

Have dreamed of escalation and an end—
An easy rise through Credits to The End,

And there, a heaped-up female ziggurat
As perfect summit to transfigure at.

A Song in Subtitles

The timeless shadow, infinite of reach,
Declines in time from silence into speech.

You, idol of our finite time and place,
Who spoke me, accent wholly without grace,

My common need and its specific steps,
Repeat them still, but only move your lips;

And all your motions, gauche or overtrained,
I have remembered. I have freed, restrained.

Such eloquence as they have now is mine.
It is the art these actors, grown pure line,

Attain through being mute; and their myth, you,
So much more pre-existent now, seem too;

Until the simple gesture (more is less)
Brings back the other side of consciousness;

And they and we, in silence beyond sound,
Re-enter what is there, or is not found.

A Song to Be Syndicated

Not nearly there, our rebirth journey wrecks.
We are the Katzenjammer Kids with sex;

And must again, in early adolescence,
Act out the dual and destructive presence.

I am Hans, dark still, still true to type.
In short, I am a shadow archetype.

You, recognizable behind your tan,
Are still incipient blond superman,

Too alien for twin, too close for brother.
But here is Mama, otherwise Great Mother,

And here the Captain—all that burgherdom
We take up arms against, and would become.

Inspector, bored *voyeur* of what old crime,
Seem rather, by your bearded visage, Time.

Break, Time, these frames and set us free: cured freaks
Borne oppositely down the strip of weeks;

I, in the flat balloons my set speech fits,
Always to say, "Auf Wiedersehen, Fritz."

A Song to Be Vindicated

A little like the *Macon*, drawing-board baroque,
An ornate rocket ship knifes through the inked-in smoke,
Her life-class pilot faceless. Is it Flash? Brick? Buck?

And in that Art Nouveau control room, also steering,
Who, golden hair marcelled and earrings wired for hearing,
Stands by with uplift bra? Intrepid Wilma Deering.

Robot sunshine, real night, robot chaperon.
Insomniac Miss Deering dials the somnatone,
Upstanding Buck has two cold showers *and* the tone.

Then, a landscape littered with the shapes of crystals,
And a perfect landing (robot luck). No hostels,
No 4–H. Wilma, the disintegrator pistols!

Hawk-men seize us, giant lizards tongue our heels.
But Hawk-man One, the brute archangel hung with seals,
Leads toward the dark skyscrapers and the upturned keels.

An architecture early Chrysler Building, bongo
Drums its sole communication, and the Congo
Model for its rule—the yellow planet Mongo:

Reprimanded by the League, and one vast press
Of war lords. If its winds seem foul, its seas are cess.
Its present emperor is Ming the Merciless.

Can lonely Ming find happiness with Earthling lover?
His torturers think yes. Can Buck, so far from clever,
Implode the anti-matter soon enough to save her?

No. But Dr. Huer's flagship lands relief,
And crowns Buck Ming the Second—jockey strap gold leaf,
His theme song Siegfried's world-inheritance motif.

Domestic Symphony

I sell securities, and am artistic.
Your career is somewhat more elastic.

Not quite viable but not quite kept,
Which would you be, if you were less inept?

I pay and cope, deny you, house, indulge.
You keep in training: swagger, ripple, bulge.

Here, in this décor layer after layer
High to middle Metro-Goldwyn-Mayer,

You are Tarzan, I am Baby Jane.
If, earlier, we each were Boy, the gain

Is both a self and other. How it came
We know already. Mother was to blame.

Blame, then, and settle down to being other:
Tell me—I'm all self—you like me rather.

Tell me that, however strained its uses,
So late a compromise at least amuses.

Tell me use will ease that act of pride
Where each is cross and each is crucified.

Say Heaven is this tree house we have sinned in.
Our wine is ready. Pour, while I fix din-din.

A Descent from San Simeon

Marion, device and balustrade
Emblazon and protect, seclude and shade;

And if the artist's shield, the builder's lime,
Alike go down before the siege of time,

We precede them—in our Packard twelves
No little of the juggernaut ourselves.

In sacrifice to my departing car
Swarm left and right the purchases we are:

Displaced sarcophagi, the forty maids,
The zebras who are equine colonnades.

Underneath your wheels, another we,
More abstract, reach the presence they will be

That have, eternal love, the empty cool
By Roman columns and the level pool;

While who desert them, sick with mortal ills,
Conclude full circle. Let these yellow hills

Consign them. You to a stammered discontent,
I to silence, then to Millicent.

You Kirsten, Me Lauritz

Divinity embarrasses, and who were gods
In retrospect seem their machine: geared clouds

The vehicle, but they, whatever they have been,
The bloated pumpkins of a past Valhalloween.

Still, when the tracking stylus inches back in time,
Shellac and vinyl, flesh, machine sublime.

Sound frees them. What remains, the might of pure intent,
However little chic, transcends embarrassment.

Will the soprano, tenor the idea, each
Has summarized the flesh to be its reach.

At the edge of strength, long after youth could think it sport,
They fake such ease as though breath were of no import;

As though, aware that breath is all, they made it youth
Forever in the late-maturing mouth

Which cares no longer—not for strength, nor youth, nor skill
Itself, except as art seems finally pure will.

Essential arrogance become the perfect self,
Illusion—you for whom all tones are twelve—

Is not and is the narrow testament we leave:
The proud specific music on the neutral stave.

It is the prop Isolde in the real attire,
Real heat behind the magic-lantern fire.

Allerseelen

At sundown, toward the island of the dead,
To whitewashed tombs among the dry palmettos,
Will come, in seasonal solicitude,
Processions of the shadowy mulattoes;
Bringing, upon the eve the soul returns,
Cut flowers to place in weathered plaster urns.

Glass-sheltered candles light them to their dead.
For them, whose surface burials distinguish
Each coffin from the grave's similitude,
Death is a yearly and specific anguish:
To seek, in dusts that earth has not combined,
Brief resurrections which they fear to find.

The dead, though they should have for sepulcher
Graves shallower than these, out of its dimness
Will not return; nor in the mind grow clear,
Nor darken subtly into final sameness;
But in the changes of the years ahead,
Remain the distant and the present dead.

A Colony of Another Kind

The engines of the carnival, Sosthène,
Become the scavengers of pestilence,
And bear to smouldering necropolis
The revelers, the carrion alike.

The women of the balconies grow old,
Or were, perhaps, transvestites from the first.
One does not care.
              The swarthy torcheliers
In double file light us toward sepulture,
And are themselves become such images
As on our tombs survive to mock our ashes:
Marabout, mulatto, octoroon,
They vaunt unquestioningly into time
The transitory kinships of the flesh.

A rising gale divides their lifted fires;
The blown confetti whitens into rain.
Papier-mâché disintegrates in wind . . .

Égalité (the little marmoset)
Trembles in his Moroccan livery.

Incompetence has closed about the chefs.

Nocturne

Together, into opposition,
Back together, swing and glider
Pendulum the idle dark.
Impatient fly and patient spider,
Now, we truce the long attrition—
Porch no longer parlor, stark
Pursuit slowed in the slowing arc.

To each late wilderness its manna.
Unemployed, except as roomer,
I will not refuse that bit,
Or fault the you whom I must humor.
In your hair the dye is henna;
In your dress the dye is Rit.
In all your house, the air is Flit.

If later, near the Negro houses,
Rags and rubber tires burn nightly,
Will their truer pesticide,
Blown here, clear off this porch completely?
And who, beyond that smoke, supposes
How, the swatter laid aside,
The hands seek on, the kill has died.

Cane Mill

In winter, through felled pines,
The clearing fills with still,
Flat haze. In blurred confines,
The lame mule turns the mill.

Sugars and resin, grain
By grain, burn toward their lees;
And where two smokes, one cane,
One pine, drift in the trees,

Dark residues foretell
Our season's heritage—
Where, through time's circling smell,
The slow mule plods toward age.

The Lumber Baron

The granite angel and the cast-iron fence
Share that neglect of death they would atone.
This gate, though it sequester decades hence
A chatelaine still wearing veils of stone,

Cannot ward off at last the toppling doom
Of seedlings rooted at her earthbound feet.
Now, young pines scent my grave with narrow bloom,
Spiced with the wood it yields. I find it sweet,

For all that I preferred to trees alone
A smell of sawmill smoke and turpentine,
The sawdust pile afire deep in its cone.
Sawdust and lumber, blood and yellow bone
That were my life, inherit from the pine,
When fires are gone, a fire, a breath not mine.

A Clock with a Mirror Face,
Presented to a Lady

Because the hemispheres of day and night
Succeed each other faster than they might,
And in that interchange of night and day
The lumens of thy beauty wear away,
I give thee, measure of a smoother change,
A little world the dark cannot derange;
That substitutes, for circling of the sun,
Slow wheels that turn all moments into one;
That marks the interdicts, the pomps of time,
With noncommittal click and neutral chime,
Till change, diffused through uniform degrees,
Diminishes in wastes of litotes.

Turn therefore, with thy fragile beauty fast,
From transiences where beauty cannot last;
From where a chronometric universe
Clocks beauty's passing and is beauty's hearse.
Turn from the frictions of the flesh and bone
And contemplate denatured change alone.
Look only in this numbered mirror face
And find a timepiece that cannot erase,
Where fixed an instant beauty's image stands
Passed over carelessly by time's two hands.

Chronology

The circling shadow on the measured dial,
The calibrated falling of the weight,
Are both time's gauge and time's discreet denial.

No captive shade, returning at its date
Unchanged, no loud imprisoned pendulum
Through changeless gravity can calculate

The unimagined change—the swift and dumb
Deforming of the days that countermands
Pursuit of time as a continuum.

Go rather to the random falling sands,
That funnel quicker with decreasing mass;
Go to a lens, that blurs what it expands;
To candles crumbling as their lusters pass;

To cold quicksilver backing mounted glass.

Ways of Feeling

Here is the opened heart, and here the Calais:
    You the letters, you the loss.
The fresh incision you, the drug, the knife.
Mine is the threatened and surrounding life.

Too radical for more than partial cure,
    The not unwelcome message, late
Revealed, at last informs. Not much a lesson
Then, you teach me now my own discretion.

Who shows the sores becomes in time the leper.
    Who, his privacy his skill,
Has learned their language, knows, if surgeons fail,
An inexhaustible and cautious braille.

Janus Redemptor

Divinity who scorn the time you are,
Who toward all past, all future, turn in pride
The arbitrary face age cannot scar,

Two-personed god, redeemer who divide,
Pity at last what ages and is whole.
Coherent in decay, its end descried,

The self which turns from that implicit goal
Denies also each turning which it is:
The continuity that were its soul.

If, closed in your one skull, two entities
Cohabit still, age now prejudging youth,
Youth given hindsight toward its own demise,

If ambiguity can pity truth,
Equivocate that truth in which I die.
Else, cleaving self from self, and so from death,

Partition quite. I whose integrity
Divides beneath that double shade you cast
Would to those alter egos, neither I,
Impute the future, delegate the past.

Kings

The double eagle of eternity,
As on their coins, upon their tombs will lie.

The mummied kings grow elegantly old.
The minted kings, worn smooth, go back to gold.

And toward that dust where both will be combined,
The timeless bird looks forward and behind.

Midas

Naught that I touched, naught that I loved grew old.
I died alone among mnemonic gold.

Distinguished contemporary poetry in cloth and paperback editions

ALAN ANSEN: *Disorderly Houses* (1961)

JOHN ASHBERY: *The Tennis Court Oath* (1962)

ROBERT BAGG: *Madonna of the Cello* (1961)

ROBERT BLY: *Silence in the Snowy Fields* (1962)

TURNER CASSITY: *Watchboy, What of the Night?* (1966)

TRAM COMBS: *st. thomas. poems.* (1965)

DONALD DAVIE: *Events and Wisdoms* (1965); *New and Selected Poems* (1961)

JAMES DICKEY: *Buckdancer's Choice* (1965) [National Book Award in Poetry, 1966]; *Drowning With Others* (1962); *Helmets* (1964)

DAVID FERRY: *On the Way to the Island* (1960)

ROBERT FRANCIS: *The Orb Weaver* (1960)

JOHN HAINES: *Winter News* (1966)

RICHARD HOWARD: *Quantities* (1962)

BARBARA HOWES: *Light and Dark* (1959)

DAVID IGNATOW: *Figures of the Human* (1964); *Say Pardon* (1961)

DONALD JUSTICE: *The Summer Anniversaries* (1960); [A Lamont Poetry Selection]

CHESTER KALLMAN: *Absent and Present* (1963)

VASSAR MILLER: *My Bones Being Wiser* (1963); *Wage War on Silence* (1960)

W. R. MOSES: *Identities* (1965)

DONALD PETERSEN: *The Spectral Boy* (1964)

HYAM PLUTZIK: *Apples from Shinar* (1959)

VERN RUTSALA: *The Window* (1964)

HARVEY SHAPIRO: *Battle Report* (1966)

JON SILKIN: *Poems New and Selected* (1966)

LOUIS SIMPSON: *At the End of the Open Road* (1963); [Pulitzer Prize in Poetry, 1964]; *A Dream of Governors* (1959)

JAMES WRIGHT: *The Branch Will Not Break* (1963); *Saint Judas* (1959)